100 Years From The

OLD MISSION

In
Grand Traverse County
Michigan

Revised Edition

by AL BARNES

Illustrations by James H. Keffer

Afterword by Larry Wakefield

ISBN 0-915937-09-3

Published by
HORIZON BOOKS, 243 E. Front St., Traverse City, MI 49684

Dedicated to the shades of the Grand Traverse Pioneers. Rest them, & may they be not too shocked at the very asinine things we moderns do and say.

PREWORD

❖

The following pages are brought together with the hope that you will like them.   We do not presume to present a history of the Grand Traverse County . . . . merely a few of the interesting highlights. If you like the story, we are thrilled, for we have tried to make it as readable and friendly as possible.

The art work is as authentic as it can be made. Photographs, when they were available, were used as a guide in making the original drawings: Where pictures were not available, no effort was spared in transposing word pictures for your enjoyment.

Thanks are due many people for their fine co-operation in the tedious search for facts. A list of their names will be found in the back of the book. As you glance through it you can be sure that each individual put his or her shoulder to the wheel and pushed mightily in one way or another.

CONTENTS

❖

ILLUSTRATIONS

CHIEF AHGOSA

CHIEF AHGOSA, son of Chief Aish-gua-gwan-aba, was given the Christian name of Addison Potts when he became converted under the teachings of Rev. Peter Dougherty. Unlike his father, Chief Ahgosa was a kindly person and likeable. Following a trip to Washington on tribal business in 1836 the Chief insisted on wearing a tall silk hat and a frock coat. It is believed this custom was impressed upon the chief's mind by his brief contact with Washington dignitaries.

Chief Ahgosa, who's name translates "the flying hawk," never became thoroughly Angelcized nor did he ever learn to handle the English language to any degree of fluency. He was tall, handsome, and intelligent and his cooperative nature made the rigid existance of the first white settlers much more bearable.

He was born at St. Clair, moving to Les Cheneaux Islands then to Charlevoix, Norwood and again southward to the central point of the Grand Traverse region that is now the Old Mission Peninsula.

The exact dates of Chief Ahgosa's birth and death are not a matter of record. It is assumed that he was born late in the seventeenth century. Following his death, the body was buried at the New Mission Cemetery in Leelanau County.

As a tribute to the young Chief Ahgosa, may it be said that he was honest and regarded a promise as a trust. He was upright in all his dealings with the white men and he grieved when they dealt otherwise with him.

Chief Aish-gua-gwan-aba, father of Chief Ahgosa, was a far cry from his likeable son. He was of a rolly-polly build and loved the 'little brown jug.' The Indian meaning of his name is "the final feather." He disliked the church because as he once said to Rev. Dougherty, "I can't go to church because when I sit down I have to smoke and I can't smoke in church." Rev. Dougherty once referred to him as an "old snake."

Chief Ahgosa

THE MOUND BUILDERS

*C*HE FIRST White settlers in the Grand Traverse Region found, along the banks of the Boardman River near the present site of the Grand Traverse County court house, a series of low burial mounds. These mounds definitely antedated the Indian occupation, proving conclusively that a people resided here centuries before the red men. While no authentic record was kept of the opening of the mounds, data gathered from similar mounds in other parts of the state would reveal that the builders undoubtedly come under the Hopewellian in the archaelogical classification and would indicate that the builders were strikingly related to the people who built the large mounds in southern Ohio.

Physically, the mounds were between three and five feet in heighth, and seventeen to twenty feet in diameter. The usual procedure of the builders was to place the body of a tribal member on the ground and then scoop a shallow trench around it, heaping the dirt toward the center.

Mention of the mounds was made by such able historians as S. E. Wait and Morgan Bates. It is possible that they were never opened, rather that they were merely leveled off and their content, along with their location lost beyond recovery.

We assume, and our assumption is borne out by statements from archaeologists of note, that the builders were a copper colored people, stalwart, with high cheek bones and jet black hair. They possessed an understading of the use of the minerals, especially copper, specimens having been found in quite some quantities in supervised mound excavations.

It is possible, that they were merely a part of the civilization that reached outward from Indiana and Ohio having its high point of perfection located in the Buck-Eye State.

However, the fact still remains that Grand Traverse County was not only the hunting ground, but the home, of a people long before its discovery by the aborigines.

INDIAN WARFARE

*I*NDIAN Warfare in Grand Traverse County has always been a subject of much discussion. Historians have it that there has never been a battle of any importance in the region. On the other hand, tradition says that a bloody struggle took place five miles east of Traverse City.

According to a composite of all available versions of the fight, the Ottawas were attacking a small tribe called the Musquetaws*, encamped on the bluff overlooking the east arm of Grand Traverse Bay.

The atackers swarmed across the arm of water in canoes and dugouts in such vast numbers that the small tribe was wiped out. No definite reason has been given for the hostilities but it is assumed, and logically so, that the Ottawas were very jealous of the excellent hunting ground of the region and resented outside tribes coming in to usurp it.

The Indian agent at Grand Rapids, then a small lumbering town, hearing rumors of the impending fray, was dispatched, posthaste, with money and blankets to buy peace. He arrived in time to turn the money and merchandise over to the Mushquetaws* and immediately dispatched a message to the camp of the Ottawas. The 'bribe' according to the story was a 'gold piece for each brave and a blanket for his squaw'.

However, before the messenger arrived in the camp, the Ottawas had decided to attack. They did, and the result was a complete annihilation of the smaller tribe.

The absolute truth of this story cannot be vouched for. Facts, to support it are: there are numerous old fire pits buried beneath vegetation in the hills above the 'five-mile-corners', an arrow manufactory was once located on the banks of Mitchell Creek; also, several burial mounds were discovered just south of the head of the bay and several south of the scene of the battle.

* Spelling variable.

THE OLD MACKINAW TRAIL

*T*HE MACKINAW TRAIL . . . . sometimes referred to as the "Indian Trail" . . . . was the connecting link between the North and the South of the state.. Nothing more than a wide footpath . . . . too narrow to permit the passage of a wagon . . . . the trail was the one artery that carried the lifeblood of civilization to the Grand Traverse Region.

The actual course of the trail is not known other than it followed the shore of the Lake to a great extent until it passed the head of Grand Traverse Bay . . . . thence it swung inland, branching to Grand Rapids and Detroit.

In the pine barrens eastward from Traverse City, within the limits of Grand Traverse County, there still remains visible marks of the trail. Worn deep by countless thousands of moccasined feet the path is all but buried under fallen leaves and rotting vegetation.

Within the limits of Traverse City there are still two gnarled trail marker trees. It was a common practice for the Indians to break or bend a sapling to designate a route. One of these trees is located on Washington Street just east of the courthouse . . . . another just outside the Northwestern Michigan fair grounds. The tree on Washington Street is appropriately marked by a bronze plaque.

The tramp of native feet cannot be heard on the old Mackinaw Trail today. The ox-team has been replaced by the tractor. The galloping pony has been superceded by the automobile and airplane. Yet . . . . comes that thrill . . . . that feeling of awe . . . . when we tramp over the trails where once Chief Ahgosa . . . . Chief Ahgosa's ancestors . . . . reigned and were revered.

ARRIVAL OF PETER DOUGHERTY

*R*EV. PETER DOUGHERTY, a graduate of the Princeton Theological Seminary, visited the Peninsula of what is now the Grand Traverse County during the summer of 1838. The purpose of his visit was to locate a place where he could build a Presbyterian mission and carry christianity to the greatest number of redmen possible. Finding considerable settlement on the Peninsula he returned to his starting point, Mackinaw City. In May 1839, with Rev. John Fleming as assistant, and four Indian oarsmen, they set out again for the chosen location.

Arriving in the little harbor at the north end of the Peninsula, Dougherty and Fleming found one lone Indian. The rest of the encampment were on the east shore of the bay on a hunting expedition. Following a conference with the one inhabitant of the camp, a smoke signal was sent up and the rest of the tribe recalled.

The Indians constructed a bark shack for the missionary's use. With the construction of a more substantial home, Rev. Dougherty dedicated his bark shack residence to the cause of education and a school was opened.

The carefully laid plans of Rev. Dougherty were disturbed before the end of June by the arrival of a messenger from Mackinaw City bearing tidings of the death of Fleming's wife. Fleming immediately set out with the four Indian oarsmen and never again returned to the Mission.

But for a small party of surveyors working in the dense forest somewhere east of Torch Lake, Peter Dougherty was the only white person in the country. Later in June Henry Schoolcraft, government agent to the Indians, Robert Graverat, interpreter, and Isaac George, blacksmith, arrived in a small boat. Peter Greensky was secured to act as an interpreter for Rev. Dougherty.

The first snow fall of 1841 found four residential log houses and one log school house in the village. In addition to this there were scores of Indian shacks sand wigwams.

THE CHURCH

*I*N THE Year of 1842 Rev. Peter Dougherty began the construction of the first frame house in Old Mission. Following the construction of the house, now known as the "Rushmore house", the Old Mission church was erected. This building constructed along the lines of the well known French Canadian buildings was of hewn timber, placed in grooved corner posts and fastened with pegs. The exact size of the church is not a matter of record but it is remembered as approximately 20' x 30'.

Over a period of years there has been considerable discussion concerning the exact location of the building. The majority of opinion, however, seems to have the location just a few rods from the sandy Old Mission beach and a short way south of the present location of the dock.

Surrounding the church was an Indian village of considerable size. The bark shacks, and wigwams covered with government cloth, were the skyscrapers and penthouses of the redmen.

The bell for the Old Mission church was cast from large British pennies donated by the Indians for this purpose. On the removal of the mission to the west side of the bay the the bell was also transported and, now at Omena, it is still in use.

The church was later moved from its location on the beach to a more accessible one, facing the highway. In this new location a stone foundation was built and the church sided. At a still later date it was razed and today nothing but the stone foundation remains as a monument to the original church.

In 1939 the Old Mission Betterment Association reorganized, after 15 years of inactivity, for the purpose of rebuilding the old house of worship. The idea being to commemorate the work and hardships of the first settlers.

REV. PETER DOUGHERTY

A TRIBUTE

*O*NLY A MAN inspired with a love for service and a hope for life in the Beyond could have expressed himself in writing and in deed as did Rev. Dougherty.

On the 29th day of June, 1839 he wrote this, in his diary; "This day laid the foundation for a second house. Aish-qua-gwan-aba and some of his people came up today. I invited them to attend our meeting. Tomorrow is the Sabbath. O that the Lord would come down by His Spirit and convert these ignorant and dying people."

On the next day, Sunday, June 30, he wrote as follows: "The morning bright and pleasant. Most of the men absent. Sent word to Aish-qua-gwan-aba, who attended worship with several of his men. Talked to them about the origin of man. All attentive."

The zeal and earnestness with which he attended his duties and the implicit faith he placed in his fellow men has been a spiritual monument to his work and an inspiration to struggling mankind.

Rev. Peter Dougherty

MRS. PETER DOUGHERTY

Van Buren, Indiana
April 20, 1939

Mr. Alonzo Barnes
Traverse City, Michigan

Dear Sir:

My Father, Rev. Peter Dougherty, was born at Newbury, New York on the Hudson River sometime in the year 1805 and died at Somers, Wis. on February 15, 1894. For some few years before attending and graduating from Princeton he was a merchant in New York City. He made his first trip to the Grand Traverse Region in 1838 and in the spring of 1839 returned and established the Old Mission, remaining there and at Omena for some 30 or 35 years. The first 12 years at Old Mission and the remainder at Omena as a missionary, teacher and preacher among the Indians. After that time he was a Presbyterian minister at Somers, Wisconsin.

My Mother, Maria Solomon Higgins Dougherty, was born in Virginia in the year 1819. Her father was a slave holder but before the war he freed his slaves and later moved to Princeton, New Jersey where my mother received her education. Mrs. Dougherty had two brothers in the Confederate Army. She died and was buried at Somers, Wisconsin in the year 1875.

Rev. Mrs. Dougherty was the mother of 9 children, eight girls and one boy, all of which have passed on except myself. Rev. Mrs. Dougherty and five of my sisters are buried at Somers, Wis. and exact dates could be found on the stones of their graves.

I have not been to Somers, Wis. for about 16 years and having no exact records have done the best I can. I hope that this will be of some help to you.

Sincerely yours,

(Signed)

Mrs. John Howard

26

Mrs. Peter Dougherty

THE LUMBER INDUSTRY

𝒯HE FIRST Sawmill in Grand Traverse County was erected by Horace Boardman in 1847. With money furnished by his father, he purchased a tract of land, now covered by the city of Traverse City, and erected a small water power mill on Mill Creek (Asylum Creek.) This mill was later (1851) purchased by Hannah, Lay & Company, enlarged and moved to the shore of the bay . . . . (Clinch Park.) Boardman's tiny mill, with its muley saw, was the progenitor of the lumbering industry in the region.

Other mills came in rapid succession. Water was soon superceded by a much more practical energy, steam, and the pine and hardwood disappeared rapidly from the county.

On the tract originally purchased by Horace Boardman stood one of the finest growth of pine to be found anywhere in the Grand Traverse region, inland were hemlock and hardwood. Hemlock was cut and stripped of its bark for the tanning industry. The logs were burned, in many cases, to get rid of them.

Some of the timber taken from the present site of Traverse City was used in the construction of a bridge across Illinois River at LaSalle, Illinois. One shipment, it is said, was used in the construction of an European Royal Palace.

The census of 1874 showed a total of 15 steam power mills in Grand Traverse County alone. Records of 1873 show an estimated cut of 25,000,000 feet of lumber. From then on there was a steady increase in the number of mills and in the number of board feet cut. In 1893 there ware 14 mills operating and the cut was estimated at 250,000,000 feet and was considered the peak of Grand Traverse County lumber industry.

The Hannah & Lay mill on the bay shore was equipped with a band saw capable of turning out 10,000,000 board feet a year. Perry Hannah once estimated the total cut from the mill at 500,000,000 feet of lumber and 250,000,000 shingles.

THE LUMBERJACKS

*T*HE MYTHICAL color and romance that is the heritage of the lumberjack will live and grow so long as there is a single descendant of that rugged and violent people who fought to tame the wilderness.

In truth, there was no beauty or romance in the workaday world of the lumberman. Unless one can construe the stench of sweating bodies, the squeak of harness leather . . . . frozen feet and fingers . . . . broken bodies . . . . beans, side pork and boiled potatoes three meals a day . . . . unless one can see beauty in those things.

Men who followed the logging operations, were not weaklings. Rather, they were the cream of the man-power crop. The rigorous life was heartless in its weeding the weak from the strong.

Bawdy songs and livid jokes were the levening elements in many of the camps. An occasional dance or maybe a wandering road show provided the balance of the social activities. Wrestling in that good old 'nothing barred' lumber-jack style helped to liven many evenings.

All-in-all, there was little time for frivolities and thoughts of romance. The working day began with the first streak of dawn and ended when the woods became sullen with darkness.

Despite the ribald tales that filter through the generations, there was something clean about the bare-knuckle brawls of the men who fought the timberline. There was something heartening about the coarse songs that echoed through the hills. Echoed . . . . and with each rebound of sound added permanence to the glory that is the woodsman's.

THE OLD BLOCKHOUSE

$\mathcal{T}$HE FIRST Building within the corporate limits of Traverse City was located on the bank of the Boardman River and was built in the year of 1847 by Horace Boardman.

Boardman, who's father had financed the purchase of 400 acres of virgin timber covering the present site of Traverse City, decided to leave his home town at Naiperville, Illinois and enter the lumbering business. After a short stop in Chicago he arrived in Grand Traverse in early June, 1847.

His first duty was to erect a shelter of some sort. The site chosen for the building at a point where Boardman Avenue joins East Eighth Street. If a stake were driven into the exact spot it would be in front of the Cigar Box Factory and just a little south of the center line of the street.

The house itself was not pretentious. It was of hewn log construction, about sixteen feet by twenty-four feet, and had but one story. The walls of the building were erected first and covered with ship's canvas and bark to protect the inhabitants until the little mill was in operation. Lumber was cut for the floor and roof during the first run of the mill.

Right back of the house was an Indian canoe landing and a motley collection of Indian wigwams. During the hunting and berry seasons the shore of the lake was popular camping grounds for the redmen.

The 'old blockhouse', as the building came to be called, was eventually destroyed by fire. The foundation remained until as late as 1885 when that, too, was removed. No marker has ever been erected to designate its location.

THE FIRST SCHOOL

$\mathcal{T}$HE FIRST School in Traverse City was located at the head of the bay on what is now Front Street, lot 4 of block 12. The building itself was a nondescript shack built by John B. Spencer and used as a stable during the logging operations in the winter of 1851 and 1852. A far cry from the modern institutions of today . . . . it had two windows, one on the east side and one on the west. A door opened to the west. The floor was rough pine boards . . . . unmatched.

Under the supervision of A. Tracy Lay, the building was renovated and furnished as well as circumstances would permit. Text books used by the pupils were any they happened to possess. Helen Goodale, daughter of Dr. D. C. Goodale, was the first teacher. This was in the year of 1863 and the pupils enrolled in the school were: George, John, Thomas, and Elizabeth Cutler, Augusta, Clarissa, and Lucius Smith, James and Jane Carmichael, Albert Norris, and Agnes Goodale.

Following her first year of teaching, Miss Goodale spent a winter of study in Chicago and returned to her duties with a fifty cent per week increase in salary.

The next summer the student body was increased by the addition of the following pupils: Jane, Belle, and Alfred Trotman, James, John, Richard, and William Garland, Melissa, Emma, and Anna Rice, Ruth Williams, and a little later Helen, Olive, Lucinda, Edward, and Charles Blakely.

The first permanent school house was built in 1855. It was located where the Park Place Hotel Annex now stands and was designated as "District No. 1."

THE MADELINE

*A*N OUTSTANDING tale of self-education is incorporated in the story of
the schooner Madeline. Manned by five young men, the boat put in at
Bowers Harbor in the fall of 1851. Three brothers, William, Michael and
John Fitzgerald, and William Bryce and Edward Chambers were the crew.

Earlier in the fall the Madeline had stopped at Old Mission and hired
S. E. Wait as teacher, then swung around to Bowers Harbor, and presumed
to turn the boat into a school. The cabin was opened and a blackboard
constructed. A window was built into the after hatch to admit light to
the hold.

Regular school hours were established and the five young men settled
down for a winter of study. Chambers was cook for the crew and as
compensation was excused from paying any part of the $20.00 monthly salary
due S. E. Wait.

Fuel to heat the cabin was transported in a boat until the bay froze
over, then sleds were used. It might be interesting to note that the bay did
not ice over until March that year.

The result of this gigantic effort in self education can best be illustrated
by following the careers of the young men involved. William Fitzgerald
was eventually appointed government inspector of hulls in Milwaukee. His
brother Michael sailed the Great Lakes for a few seasons and purchased a
farm near Port Huron. The younger brother, John, eventually came to own
a shipyard in Milwaukee. Last record of Chambers found him light keeper
at White Fish Point. Nothing is known regarding the later life of Bryce
but it is assumed that he followed the trade of a sailor.

A small bronze plaque at Bowers Harbor sets forth the facts concerning
the "school of the inland sea."

THE MADELINE

PERRY HANNAH

*H*IS NAME Linked with that of Tracy Lay, Perry Hannah was one of the outstanding men responsible for the growth and prosperity of the Grand Traverse Region.

He was born in Erie County, Pennsylvania, on September 22, 1824. Following the death of his mother, when he was three years old, his father moved to Michigan. At the age of 13 years, Perry joined his father in the lumbering business.

In 1846 he went to Chicago and worked for one Jacob Beidler . . . . a lumber broker. With the financial aid of his employer the firm Hannah, Lay & Company was organized in the Grand Traverse Region.

In 1852 he married Miss Anna Flint. Two daughters and a son were born to this union. Mrs. Hannah died in 1898 and Mr. Hannah died on August 13, 1904.

Perry Hannah

A. TRACY LAY

A. TRACY LAY was one of the outstanding pioneers in the building of the Grand Traverse Region. He was born in Batavia, Jessee County, York State on the 18th of June, 1825.

At the age of 16 years he quit school and began work in a small rural store. In 1849 he journeyed to Chicago, soon becoming interested in the lumber industry. He formed a partnership association with a man named Perry Hannah and in 1853, with the assistance of an engineer named Thomas Whelphy, he layed out the city of Traverse City. At the same time he worked toward the organization of Grand Traverse County.

Mr. Lay married Katherine Smith on February 20, 1855. They had four daughters.

Mrs. Lay died on February 27, 1907 and Mr. Lay died on March 19, 1918.

Throughout his business career he was undoubtedly one of the most enthusiastic boosters the Grand Traverse Region has ever known. While the major part of his residence was in Chicago, he made frequent visits to Traverse City and the work he did helped to build a permanent community.

A. Tracy Lay

A HUNDRED YEARS

A HUNDRED years has been a long time. Within a century Grand Traverse County has wrested itself from the vastness of a gigantic wilderness and has grown to become a charming community . . . . a community where neighbors are friends and guests are neighbors.

From the ashes of the great forest has sprung a community that is known from one end of the continent to the other for its loveliness and natural beauty. The Grand Traverse Region has stepped from the swaddling clothes of a boomtown into the royal purple of one of the finest resort centers in the nation.

Cool breezes swirl across the rolling hillsides in summer and abundant rainfall tempers the good earth to garnish it with lush verdure of countless species.

Lakes . . . . scores of lakes dot the region. Emerald green . . . . dashing blue . . . . brilliantly debonaire in the scalding red of glorious summer sunsets.

Where once the ox-cart trundled its halting way across the plains, now giant aircraft roar overhead . . . . locomotives scream on shimmering steel . . . . automobiles whirl silently over gleaming pavements.

Traverse City, capital city of Grand Traverse County, has a year around population of over 13,000 people. Located at the head of Grand Traverse bay, it has geographically, an altitude of 612 feet above sea level, longitude 83° 30″ west, latitude, 44° 15″ north.

Mute testimony to the friendliness of the people in the place is the fact that the population of Grand Traverse County is approximately doubled during the summer months.

Industry in the county is confined primarily to fruit culture and potato growing. Following closely are dairy products and grains.

Manufacturing within the city of Traverse City is varied and employs a large percent of the year around inhabitants.

Transportation facilities include railroad connections to all larger centers as well as air transportation to all points on the continent. Modern concrete highways connect and crisscross over the entire region.

The slogan of the county, "The Heart of Nature's Playground," has come to be more than just a slogan. It is a dinner subject in the homes of the nation's vacationers.

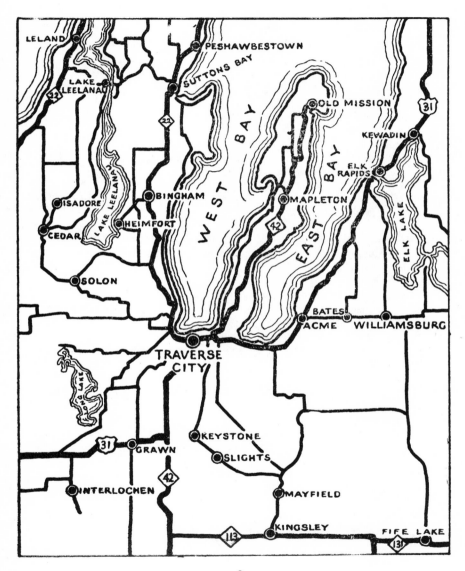

FAMOUS FIRSTS

IN GRAND TRAVERSE COUNTY

THE FIRST white settlers in Grand Traverse County were Rev. Peter Dougherty and John Fleming. 1839.

THE FIRST frame building was constructed at Old Mission by Rev. Peter Dougherty. 1842.

THE FIRST school house in Grand Traverse County was south of the We-que-tong Club. School was held in an abandoned stable during the winter of 1853.

THE FIRST school teacher was Miss Helen R. Goodale, daughter of Dr. D. C. Goodale.

THE FIRST mail service to the county was in June 1849 and consisted of two letters and a religious magazine, delivered by John Campbell.

THE FIRST steamer to enter the bay was the Michigan on April 14, 1851.

THE FIRST Post Office was established in 1851 at Old Mission. W. R. Stone, postmaster . . . salary, nothing. Mail kept in an empty raisin box nailed to the wall in the stone kitchen.

THE FIRST mail from the south was delivered by Indian Jake Ta-pa-sah in 1853.

THE FIRST wedding in Grand Traverse County was that of Olive Dame to Ansel Salisbury of Wisconsin in the fall of 1842.

FAMOUS FIRSTS

THE FIRST white child born in the county was Henry L. Miller, son of Mr. and Mrs. Lewis Miller in 1846.

THE FIRST white settlers in Traverse City were Horace Boardman and Michael Gay in 1847.

THE FIRST church constructed in Grand Traverse County was in 1842 at Old Mission.

THE FIRST civic organization of record in the county was "The Mutual Admiration Society."

THE FIRST mercantile establishment was the Hannah & Lay Co., "Dealers in everything."

THE FIRST residence in Traverse City was built in 1847 at the foot of Boardman Lake.

THE FIRST bridge constructed across the Boardman River was just south of 8th Street and was built of poles. 1847.

THE FIRST steam sawmill was erected in 1852 by Hannah, Lay & Co.

THE FIRST marriage ceremony in Traverse City was that of James Lee and Ann Dukin in 1853.

THE FIRST white child born in Traverse City was Josephine Gay, daughter of the Michael Day's on May 15, 1849.

THE FIRST white death recorded in the county was in 1852 and was a logging camp accident. No funeral services.

THE FIRST Sunday School in Traverse City started in 1853.

BIBLIOGRAPHY

In compiling the forgoing text much credit is due the following individuals and organizations for their splendid cooperation and for their assistance in verifying materials at hand. Without their many kindnesses this work would be of no more value and no more authentic than many of the newspaper creations called 'legends':

Mrs. Susan Aghosa
Ruth Cracker
"History of the Grand Traverse Region"
by Dr. M. L. Leach.
Dr. E. F. Greenman, Museum of Anthropology,
University Museums, Ann Arbor, Michigan.
State Library at Lansing, Michigan.
George Snyder
Mrs. William Hobbs
Edmund Littell
Traverse City Chamber of Commerce
Old Mission Betterment Association
George Tuttle
Jud Cameron
Traverse City Record Eagle
Mrs. John Howard
Captain George Johnson
George Eikey
Harry Brinkman
George Bates
Wm. Darrow.
Hermoine Hendryx.

AFTERWORD

❖

A Pocket History of Traverse City and Environs

This piece is not meant to upstage Al Barnes's excellent book. It is rather to update and amplify it with a more detailed account of the Traverse City area's rich history.

Most northern Michigan towns grew up around a sawmill—pine lumber gave them birth. Traverse City was no exception. It got started in 1847, when Captain Harry Boardman, a prosperous farmer near Naperville, Illinois, bought 200 acres of virgin pine timber at the foot of Grand Traverse Bay and furnished his son, Horace, with the means to build a sawmill there. Horace and two or three hired hands sailed north from Chicago in his father's sloop, *Lady of the Lake*, and arrived on the site in early June.

With the help of local Indians they finished the sawmill in October of that same year. It stood on the small creek (successively known as Mill Creek, Asylum Creek and Kid's Creek) that empties into the Boardman River at its western loop on Wadsworth Street. The only other settlement in the vast wilderness for miles around was an Indian mission near the tip of the peninsula that separates the two arms of Grand Traverse Bay. It had been established in 1839 by a Presbyterian missionary, Reverend Peter Dougherty.

The little Boardman mill continued to operate through the winter of 1850-51 but the results were disappointing. With its single muley saw, the mill was slow and inefficient, and when the price of pine lumber plummeted   in 1850 Captain Boardman (the military title was honorary) decided to sell. He found a buyer in the newly organized Chicago lumber firm of Hannah, Lay & Company and its three youthful partners Perry Hannah, Albert Tracy Lay, and James Morgan. Eager to develop their own timber resources, Hannah and William Morgan (brother of James) accompanied Captain Boardman to Grand Traverse Bay aboard the schooner *Venus* in the spring of 1851 and closed the deal. For $4,500 they acquired the sawmill and several small buildings, and the 200 acres upon which Traverse City now stands.

It is said that Captain Boardman was astonished upon arrival to find the mill shut down and all hands playing cards. Horace's explanation that he'd given his men the day off because of a threat of rain convinced the Captain that his decision to sell the property was wise.

The Hannah, Lay company lost no time in building a much larger steam mill on the Bay just west of the river's mouth. Over the next 35 years it would harvest more than 500 million feet of pine lumber in the Boardman River valley. The lumber was shipped to company headquarters in Chicago in the company's own bottoms—some of it was used to help rebuild Chicago after the Great Fire of 1871—and great wealth flowed into the pockets of all four partners. (William Morgan had been added to the partnership in 1852.)

For the first few years Hannah and Lay alternated every six months as company head in Chicago and Traverse City, but after 1855 Hannah took sole charge of affairs in Traverse City and Tracy Lay remained in the Windy City.

The village was laid out by Tracy Lay in 1852, and was granted a post office in 1853. During the winter the mail was carried weekly from

Manistee in a backpack by an Indian called Old Joe. The first school was established in 1853 with 15 year old Helen Goodale, daughter of Traverse City's first physician, David C. Goodale, as teacher. It was housed in a little log shanty, formerly a stable, on the south side of Front Street, just east of Boardman Avenue.

For the first 15 years, the tiny village was completely isolated from the outside world except by boat, and not even boat in the winter. Perry Hannah, elected to the State Legislature in 1854, had to make the trip to Lansing that winter on snowshoes, accompanied by an Indian guide. It took them ten days.

The first road south, the Northport-Newaygo State road, was opened in 1864, closely following an old Indian trail. That helped some, but Traverse City's big breakout was the coming of the first railroad, Grand Rapids & Indiana, on November 15, 1872. Whistles blew and church bells rang and people danced in the street. "Out of the Woods at Last", trumpeted the Grand Traverse Herald in banner headlines.

Henry D. Campbell, who had established the first stagecoach lines in the 1860s, built Traverse City's first big hotel, the Park Place, in 1873. The city became a railroad center with the coming of the Chicago & West Michigan in 1890 and the Manistee & Northeastern in 1892. It was incorporated as a village in 1881, and as a city in 1895, Perry Hannah elected president of both. Even during his lifetime Hannah was called the "Father of Traverse City". City water, electricity, and gas lines were established by Henry D. Campbell in the late 1880 and 1890s. The population reached almost 10,000 in 1890—a ten year gain of 116%.

But dark clouds had already began to gather on the horizon. Pine timber was depleted by 1895, and by 1915 so were the hardwoods. Also in decline were the city's mainstay industries based on wood and wood by-products. Its largest employer, Oval Wood Dish Company, for example, pulled up stakes and moved to Tupper Lake, NY, taking with it at least 100 worker families and plunging the area into an economic decline that lasted until World War II, when the town seemed empty with all its young men gone, some of whom died in battle and were gone forever.

Traverse City actually lost population in the 1920s and stagnated in the 1930s. The city was partly sustained during this period by the Northern Michigan Asylum (later called Traverse City State Hospital) under its legendary Dr. James Decker Munson, established in 1881. Over the course of the next 70 years the hospital employed an average of 1,000 people while caring for an estimated 50,000 patients.

But the seeds of resurgence had been sown as early as the 1890s, when the first commercial fruit farms were established and summer people from downstate Michigan, Ohio, and Illinois began to spend their vacations at resorts on Grand Traverse Bay and the inland lakes. Tourism and fruit farming led the way to Traverse City's phenomenal growth during the last half of the 20th century, making it the "World's Cherry Capital" with its annual National Cherry Festival, and one of the nation's prime tourist attractions.

Over time Traverse City has also become northern Michigan's center for medical care, communications, banking, insurance, government and legal services, which, along with its spectacular natural beauty, have made it one of the most desirable places in the country to live.

Now, faced with accelerated growth and development, it has become the primary task of its people to keep it that way.

—Larry Wakefield